Book 13   The trip   er

Colour this.   Write.

   er   er   er   er   er   er

                               ___ ___ ___ ___ ___ ___

riv**er**

Can you read these words?

letter   summer   her   under   dinner

Now can you read these words?   They all end with **er**.

1. boxer   2. chopper   3. drummer

4. ladder   5. slipper   6. robber

Now draw the words in these six boxes.

1. 	2.	3.
4.	5.	6.

Add **er** to finish these words.

dust __ __   j __ __ k   temp __ __   p __ __ ch   sist __ __
fish __ __ man

Can you read them?

3

Now write these words. The dashes will help you.

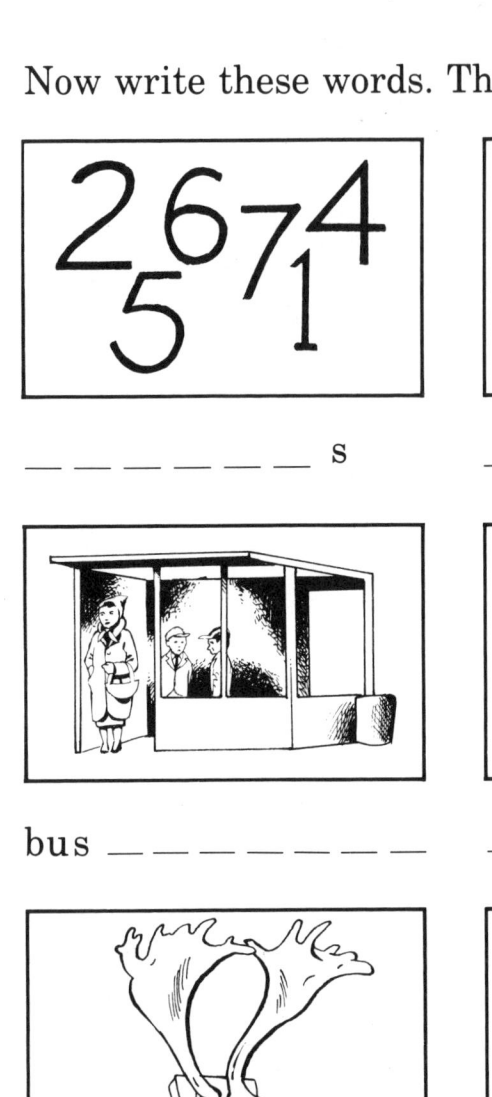
_ _ _ _ _ _ s

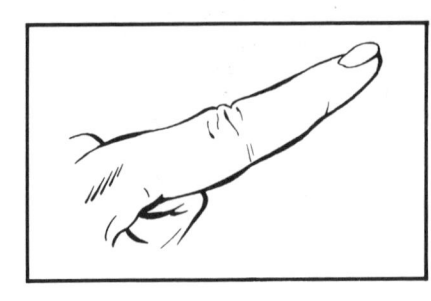
_ _ _ _ _ _

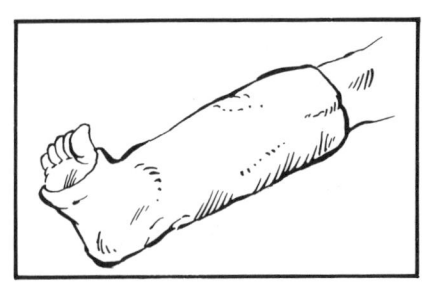
_ _ _ _ _

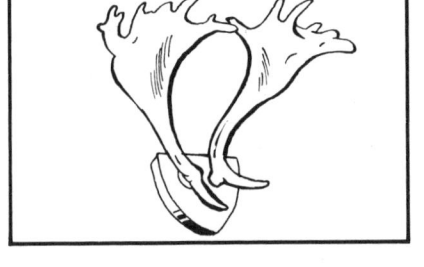
bus _ _ _ _ _ _ _ _

_ _ _ _ _ _

_ _ _ _ _ s

_ _ _ _ _ _ s

_ _ _ _ _ _

_ _ _ _ _ _

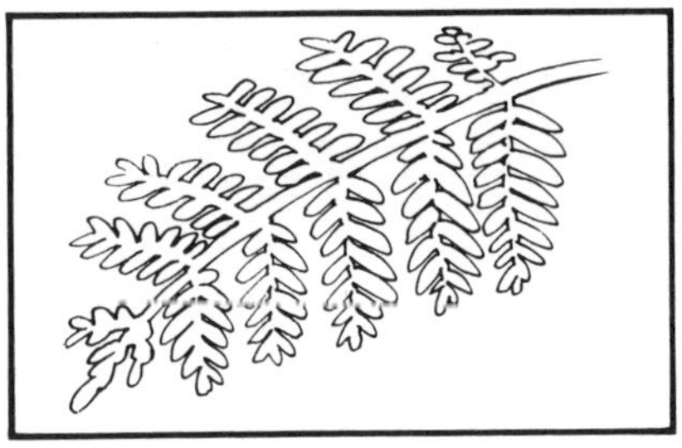

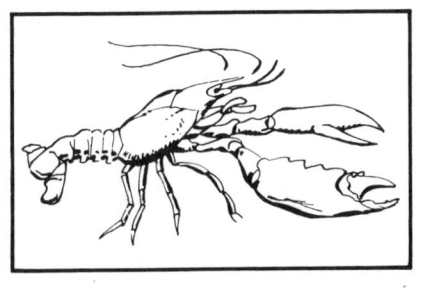
_ _ _ _

_ _ _ _ _ _

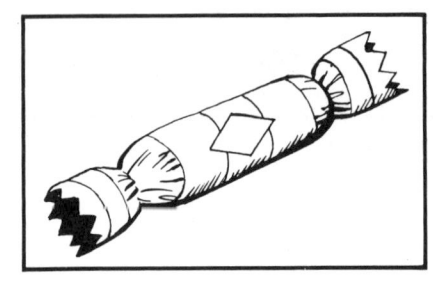
_ _ _ _ _

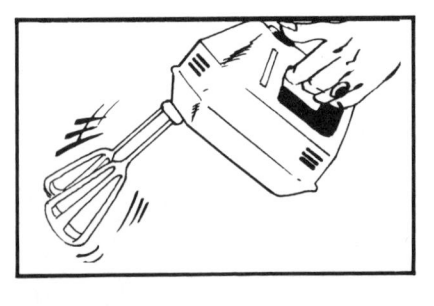
_ _ _ _ _ _

_ _ _ _ _ _

4

Draw these things.

a person sitting in a helicopter	a parrot on its perch	a fisherman catching a lobster
a fern in a plant pot	a litter bin full of litter	a picnic hamper full of good things to eat
a monster eating its supper	a man on a stretcher with his leg in plaster	a boxer dog fetching a slipper
a man up a ladder with a hammer in his hand	a man sprinkling pepper on his dinner	a chopper stuck in a log

Read these words.

spanners   letter   glitter   flippers   bigger   butter

shiver   choppers   numbers   litter   plaster   dinner

Now write them in these gaps.

1. If you polish silver it will _____.

2. You must not drop _____. Put it in the bin.

3. In America, helicopters are called _____.

4. You put _____ on sandwiches.

5. Dad gets his _____ out so he can mend his van.

6. A frogman puts _____ on to help him to swim faster.

7. If you cut a finger you must put a sticking _____ on it.

8. If you undress in winter you will _____.

9. Big Ben is _____ than Little Don.

10. If you get a present you must write a thank-you _____.

11. We are having fish and chips for _____.

12. 1, 2, 3, 4, 5 are all _____.

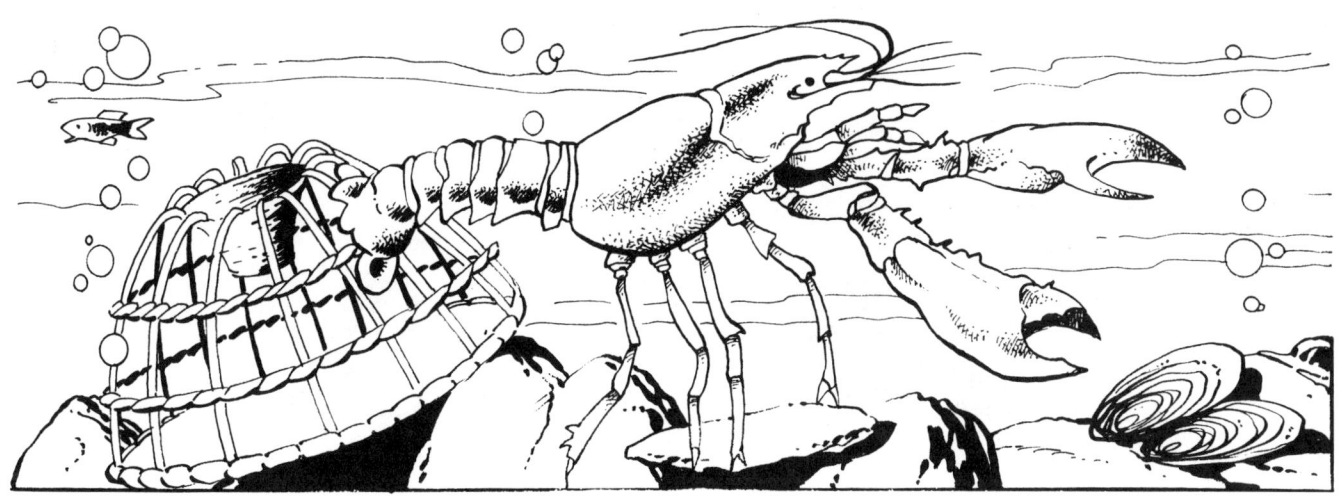

This is a lobster. It lives under rocks. It has two big nippers. These nippers are for catching fish and for digging up clams. Clams are shellfish. They live under the mud. Fishermen catch lobsters in lobster pots. They pull up the pots and get the lobsters out as fast as they can. Then they fix rubber bands on the lobster's nippers. Now the lobster cannot nip the fisherman's fingers. The fishermen drop the lobsters into big boxes. They put wet sacks on top of them so they will still live. The fishermen sell the lobsters to the fish-seller.

1. Where do lobsters live?

_____

2. What do they eat?

_____

3. Why do fishermen put rubber bands on the lobster's nippers?

_____

Draw a lobster in a lobster pot.

oo

Colour these drawings.

b**oo**t    g**oo**d

Write.   oo   oo   oo   oo   oo   oo

                                             ___ ___ ___ ___ ___ ___

All these words have **oo** in them.   Can you read them?

1. hoop   2. moon   3. stool   4. broomstick

5. wood   6. wool   7. hood   8. footprint

Now draw them in these boxes.

1.	2.	3.	4.
5.	6.	7.	8.

Add **oo** to finish these words.

b __ __ m   sc __ __ p   b __ __   h __ __ k   w __ __ d   s __ __ t

Can you read them?

8

Write the words. The dashes will help you.

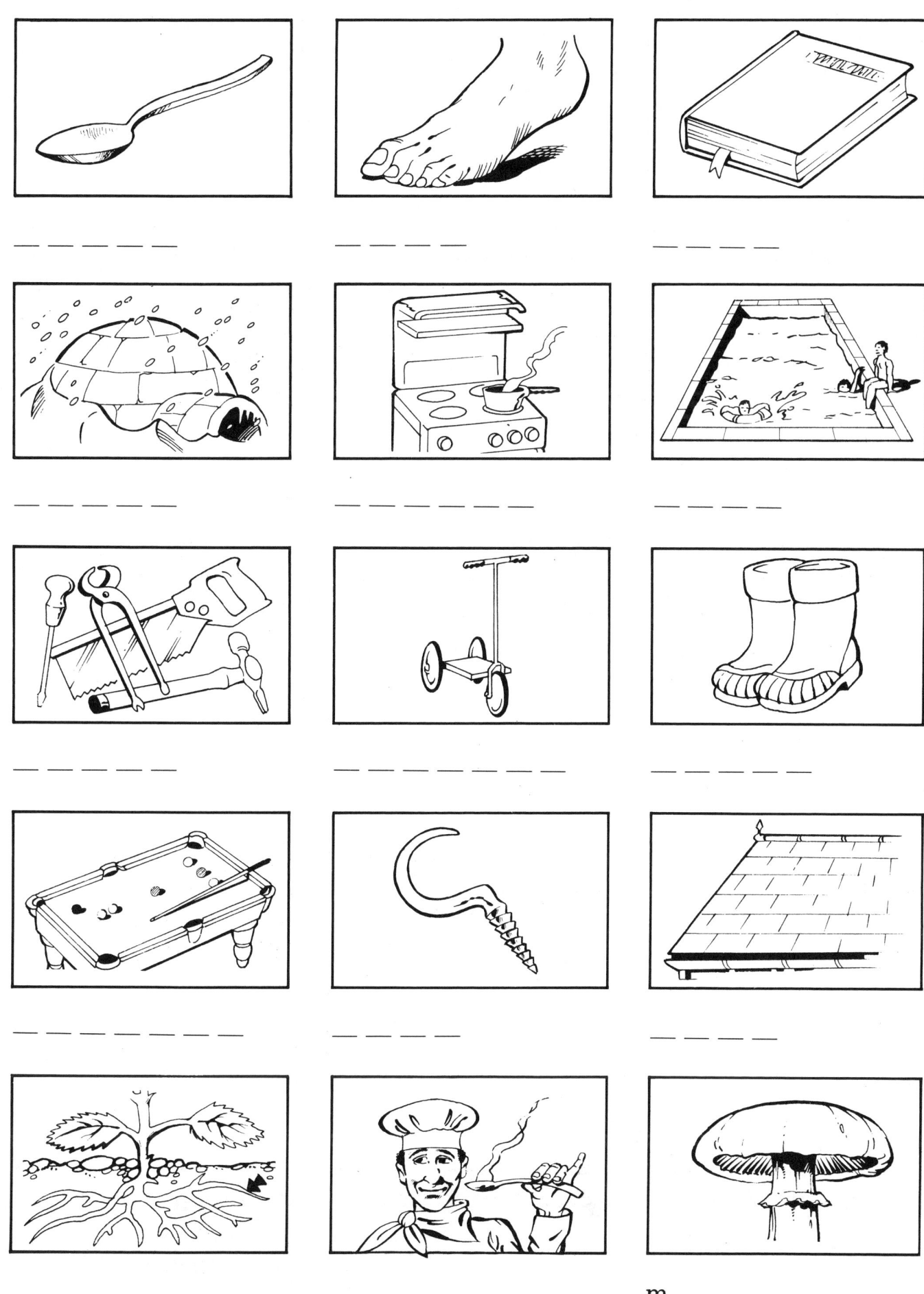

Draw these things.

a food mixer in a kitchen	a scooter with a hooter	a cook with a wooden spoon
a spook on a roof	two men playing snooker	an animal that gives us wool
a fox in a wood	a man with a boot on one foot	a man looking at a book
a room full of balloons	a box full of tools	a witch going past the moon on a broomstick

Read these words.

Blood   stool   broomsticks   crook   spoon   zoo
tooth   hook   cooker   mood   Soot   pool

Now write them in these gaps.

1. You can cook the dinner on an electric _____.

2. If you have a bad _____ you must visit the dentist.

3. If you are grumpy, you are in a bad _____.

4. We can sit on a wooden _____.

5. The fishing rod has a _____ on one end.

6. You can see lots of different animals in a _____.

7. _____ is black.

8. The _____ had a sack full of loot.

9. We swim in a swimming _____.

10. You eat milk pudding with a _____.

11. Witches travel on _____.

12. _____ is red.

This is Basher, the boxing kangaroo. He is a very clever boxer. He is going to have a contest with a man called Bad Jack. As soon as the bell goes, Basher jumps up from his stool and zooms across the ring. He swoops down on Bad Jack and hits him with a left hook.
     Thump!
Down goes Bad Jack. They have to put him on a stretcher. Basher is the winner. He is in a good mood. He thinks he is the champion.

1. What is the kangaroo called?

_____

2. What is the man called?

_____

3. Who wins the contest?

_____

4. What do the boxers sit on?

_____

y

Colour this.

happ**y**

Write.

y y y y y y

__ __ __ __ __ __

Can you read these words?

every   slippery   very   grumpy

Now can you read these words? They all end with the letter **y**.

1. dummy   2. jelly   3. lorry

4. sunny   5. holly   6. piggy bank

Draw them in these boxes.

1.	2.	3.
4.	5.	6.

Add **y** to finish these words.

boss__   hand__   luck__   lump__   cop__   mist__

Can you read them?

13

Write the words. The dashes will help you.

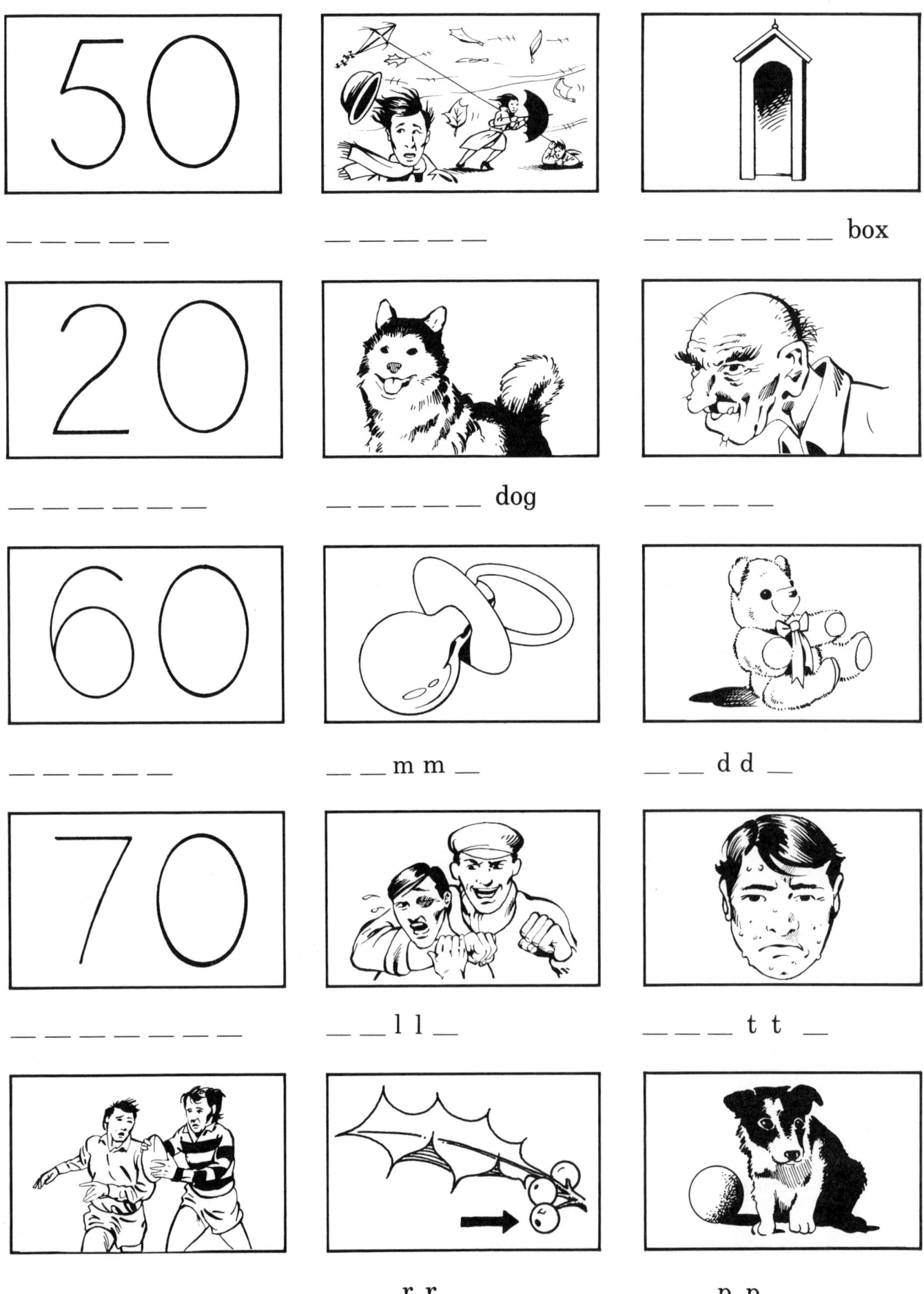

Draw these things.

an empty bath tub	some prickly holly	a black puppy in a brown basket
an angry man and a happy man	a floppy rag doll in a frilly dress	a droopy plant in a plant pot
an ugly man with a silly hat on	a messy lad with filthy hands	a scruffy tramp sitting on the back of a lorry
a frosty garden in winter	a man in muddy boots	Humpty-Dumpty

Read these words.

jolly   fizzy   prickly   Husky   crafty   twenty

smelly   sorry   clumsy   hobby   skinny   hurry

Now write them in these gaps.

1. _____ dogs live in Greenland.

2. If you bump into someone you must tell them that you are _____.

3. Two tens are _____.

4. If you are in a rush, you are in a _____.

5. A bad egg is very _____.

6. If you are very, very thin you are _____.

7. If you drop things, and bump into things, you are _____.

8. Stamp collecting is a _____.

9. Holly is very _____.

10. If someone is happy, they are _____.

11. If you are cunning, you are _____.

12. Orange pop is _____.

This is Tricky Dicky.
He has a funny hobby.
He loves to play nasty
tricks on everybody.
He puts on ugly masks,
then he jumps out at you.
What a nasty shock!
He has a floppy plastic
insect on a string.

He has a wobbly rubber frog. He puts itchy stuff down the necks of
his pals. They think he is a silly fool. He puts pepper on their food.
He puts everyone into a bad mood.

Draw an ugly mask.

Draw a floppy plastic insect.

Draw a wobbly rubber frog.

Draw a lad with itchy stuff down his back.

 As soon as you can read **Words 1** at the back
you can go on to read '**The trip**'.

17

Book 14 The Glen of Gloom

ee

Colour this.

tree

Write.

ee   ee   ee   ee   ee   ee

___   ___   ___   ___   ___   ___

Can you read these words?

see   green   sleep   creeps

All these words have **ee** in them. Can you read them?

1. street   2. coffee   3. weed

4. settee   5. sheet   6. sixteen

Draw them in these boxes.

1.	2.	3.
4.	5.	6.

Add the letters **ee** to finish these words.

d __ p   fr __   sn __ zing   yipp __   f __ l

Can you read them?

18

Write the words. The dashes will help you.

Draw these things.

a man sweeping the street	a steep, green hill	three conker trees
a sheep with very thick wool	a black and yellow bee	a chest freezer full of food
a packet of sweets	an eel on a fisherman's hook	a zoo-keeper feeding a chimpanzee
a creepy-looking monster with fifteen green teeth	a cat sleeping under a tree	a garden full of green weeds

Read these words.

weeds   deep   evergreen   Steel   peel   week

sweep   settee   teeth   greedy   freezes   Bees

Now write them in these gaps.

1. The dentist looks after _____ .

2. You must _____ an orange before you eat it.

3. If you cannot swim do not jump into the swimming pool at the _____ end.

4. If you eat lots and lots of sweets you must be _____ .

5. You must pull up the _____ from the garden.

6. _____ is a metal.

7. You can sit on a _____ .

8. There are seven days in one _____ .

9. _____ can sting you.

10. Get a broom and _____ up that mess.

11. Holly is an _____ tree.

12. In winter, the milk _____ solid.

Robin Hood went to live in Sherwood Forest because he did not agree with the King of England. The king was a greedy man and he took Robin's house and land and kept it for himself. Robin did not live in the woods by himself. He had a band of men. They were called Robin Hood and his Merry Men. They all had green outfits. They hid in the trees so they could not be seen. Robin's biggest enemy was called the Sheriff of Nottingham. But Robin Hood was much too clever for the Sheriff to catch.

1. Where did Robin go to live?

_____

2. What did the king do to Robin?

_____

3. What were Robin and his band called?

_____

4. What was Robin's biggest enemy called?

_____

5. Why was Robin difficult to see?

_____

Colour Robin's outfit. Colour it green.

ow

Colour this.  Write.

ow   ow   ow   ow   ow   ow

___ ___ ___ ___ ___ ___

do**w**n

Can you read these words?

how brown now

All these words have **ow** in them. Can you read them?

1. town   2. towel   3. sunflower

4. tower   5. dressing gown   6. trowel

Draw them in these boxes.

1.	2.	3.
4.	5.	6.

Add **ow** to finish these words.

gr __ l   p __   c __ slip   f __ l   w __   p __ er

Can you read them?

23

Write the words. The dashes will help you.

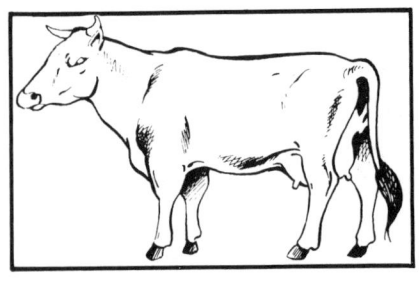  

_ _ _   _ _ _ _ _ _   _ _ _

 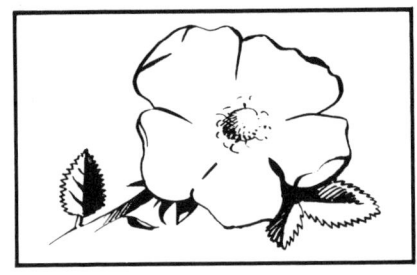 

_ _ _ _ _   _ _ _ _ _ _   _ _ _ _ _ _ ing

  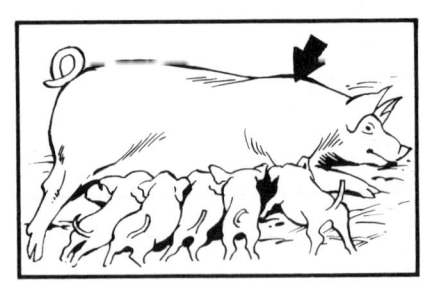

_ _ _ _ _   _ _ _   _ _ _ _ _

 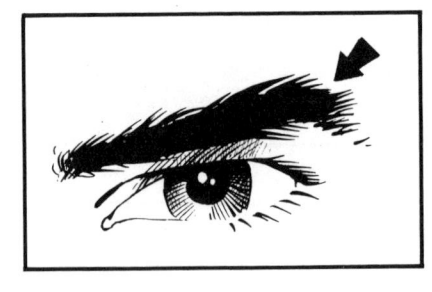 

_ _ _ _   _ _ _ _ _ _   _ _ _ _ _

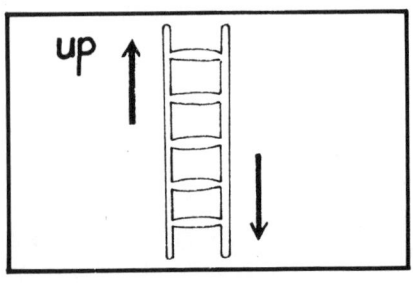 

_ _ _ _   _ _ _ _ _

Draw these things.

a clown bowing down

a brown cow in a shower

a gardener digging up some
flowers with a trowel

a king with a crown and
a dressing gown

an angry man scowling
at a little lad

a powerful man ripping a
thick book into two

a brown owl sitting down
on top of a tower

Jack and Jill tumbling down
the hill

a tin of talcum powder

a sow with seven little piglets

Read these words.

tower   How   growl   drowsy   towel   town
flowers   Owls   trowel   crown   Clowns   cows

Now write them in these gaps.

1. _____ do you do?

2. Could you lend me a _____ and trunks for the swimming lesson?

3. Dogs _____ if they get angry.

4. Mum goes into _____ to do the weekly shopping.

5. If you feel _____, you feel very sleepy.

6. A _____ is a garden tool.

7. We get milk from _____ .

8. Some _____ smell sweet.

9. The king puts on his _____ .

10. _____ go twit-twoo.

11. _____ dress up so they look funny.

12. At Blackpool there is a very big _____ .

This man has an interesting job. He is called Pow-Wow the Clown. He visits lots of towns and all the children love him. Before he goes on, he has to get ready. He puts powder on his skin and lipstick on his lips to give him a big grin. Now he puts a funny wig on, then a floppy hat with a droopy flower. He gets into a baggy dressing gown with big patches on it, then he puts big brown boots on his feet.
Now he is ready to go out and have some fun with the big crowd of children.

1. What is the clown called?

_____

2. What is on his hat?

_____

3. What colour are his boots?

_____

Draw Pow-Wow with his full outfit on.

ay

Colour this.   Write.

ay   ay   ay   ay   ay   ay

__ __ __ __ __ __

pl**ay**

All these words have **ay** in them. Can you read them?

hay   away   sway   may   say   stay

Add the letters **ay** to finish off these words, then write them under the proper box.

pl __ __   s d __ __   l __ __   pl __ __ ful   w __ __   str __ __

Hens _____ these.

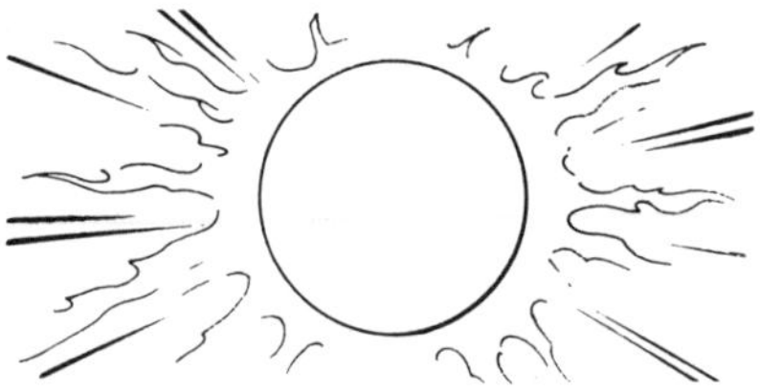

It comes up every _____ .

She _____ tennis.

This tells you the _____ .

This cat is a _____ .

He is very _____ .

28

Write the words. The dashes will help you.

_ _ _ _   _ _ _ _   _ _ _ _

 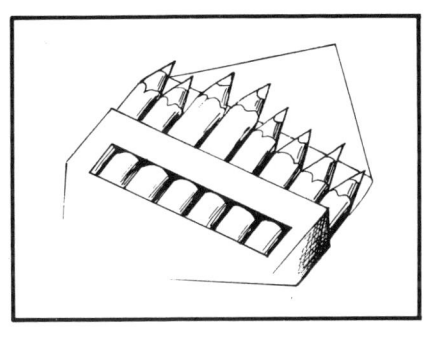 

hip-hip-hoo _ _ _ _   _ _ _ _ _ _ _   _ _ _ _ _

_ _ _ _ out   _ _ _ _ _   _ _ _ _ _

_ _ _ _ _ house   _ _ _   brick _ _ _ _ _ _

Draw these things.

a tin of red spray

a blue crayon

six lads playing cricket

a tray with some food on it

a family going off on holiday

a cow eating hay

a lorry in a layby

a subway going under a street

something that hens lay

a cat running away from a dog

a soccer player with the number three on his back

a kiln full of clay pots

Read these words.

pay   Sunday   rays   days   crayons   lay
bricklayer   way   holiday   say   tray   clay

Now write them in these gaps.

1. In summer, the sun's _____ are very hot.

2. Hens _____ eggs.

3. There are seven _____ in one week.

4. How much do you have to _____ to get into the swimming baths?

5. Go and get a packet of _____ so you can colour in that drawing.

6. _____ is the day of rest.

7. There's no _____ out of prison.

8. The potter needs lots of _____ for his pots.

9. A _____ puts up houses.

10. If I am ill, and have to stay in bed, mum brings the dinner on a _____ .

11. In the summer we get six weeks _____ .

12. What did you _____ ?

These three men are not on holiday. The ship they were travelling on hit a rock yesterday and sank to the bottom. They had to get away by swimming. Luckily, they did not drown. Now they are castaways. They may have to stay here for days and weeks. They have to catch their food. One of the men has got a fishing rod. If he doesn't catch a fish they will have to stay hungry. If no-one comes to help them soon they will have to cut down some trees for a raft.

1. Are these men on holiday?

2. Why did their ship sink?

3. What may they have for dinner?

4. How may the men get away?

As soon as you can read **Words 2** at the back you can go on to read '**The Glen of Gloom**'.

| Book 15. The snagron | ea |

Colour this.   Write.

ea   ea   ea   ea   ea   ea

eat   ___ ___ ___ ___ ___ ___

All these words have **ea** in them. Can you read them?

1. sea   2. teacher   3. team   4. seat   5. flea

6. stream   7. heater   8. cream   9. leapfrog

Draw them in these boxes.

1.	2.	3.
4.	5.	6.
7.	8.	9.

Add **ea** to finish off these words.

__ __ ch   sn __ __ k   gl __ __ m   tr __ __ t   w __ __ k

Can you read them to the teacher?

33

Draw these things.

a leaf from a holly tree	a lad eating an Easter egg	a wooden seat
a heap of blue and red beads	a seal swimming in the sea	a black cat with gleaming yellow eyes
a butcher cutting some meat	a cream jug next to a teapot	a heap of sand on the beach
a leaking bucket	a dog sneaking up on a cat	a duck with a fish in its beak

Read these words.

Seals   easy   beats   lead   bleat   flea
leader   heal   steam   neatly   meals   cheap

Now write them in these gaps.

1. You must keep your dog on a _____.

2. _____ live in the sea.

3. If you heat up some water it will begin to _____.

4. Hens cluck, pigs grunt and sheep _____.

5. Macfuzz the buzz is the _____ of the clan.

6. If it does not cost a lot, it must be _____.

7. Dinner, tea and supper are all _____.

8. The teacher said that we must write _____.

9. If it is not difficult, it must be _____.

10. A _____ is a very little insect.

11. The drummer _____ his drum.

12. If you cut yourself, put some cream on to help it to _____ up.

This little animal is a hunter and a killer. It can run up tree trunks, leap across streams and swim across rivers. The weasel tracks down and kills lots of different animals. Some of these animals live in tunnels. The weasel has a long thin body, so it is easy to creep into tunnels. The weasel grips its victims in its mouth full of gleaming teeth. If a weasel is very hungry, it will sneak up into a tree and steal some eggs from a nest. In spring, the weasel has its breeding season. It has a litter of little ones. Little weasels are called kittens. As the kittens get bigger, mum and dad teach them how to hunt.

1. Can weasels swim?

2. Why is it easy for weasels to get down tunnels?

3. Why do weasels sneak up into trees?

4. What are little weasels called?

37

ou

Colour this.    Write.

out

ou ou ou ou ou ou

___ ___ ___ ___ ___ ___

Add **ou** to finish off these words, then write each one under the proper box.

l _ _ d   c _ _ nt   undergr _ _ nd   bloodh _ _ nd   tr _ _ t   _ _ ting

This is very _____ .

This is a _____ .

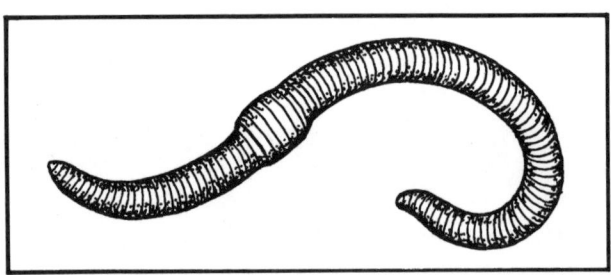

This lives _____ .

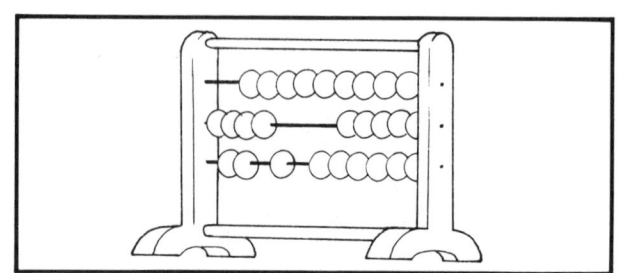

You _____ with this.

This fish is called a _____ .

They are going on an _____ .

38

Write the words. The dashes will help you.

  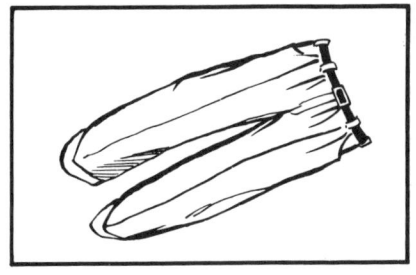

_ _ _ _ _   _ _ _ _ _   _ _ _ _ _ _ _

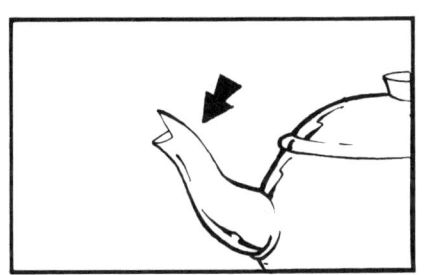  

_ _ _ _ _   _ _ _ _ _ _ _ _   _ _ _ _ _ _

  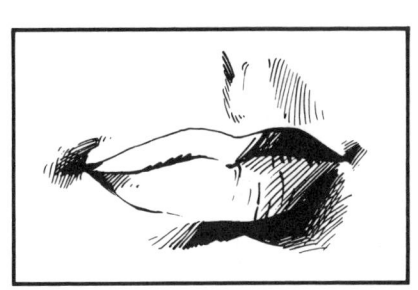

_ _ _ _ _ _ _ _ _   _ _ _ _ _   _ _ _ _

_ _ _ _ _   _ _ _ _ _ _ _   _ _ _ _ _ _ _ _

 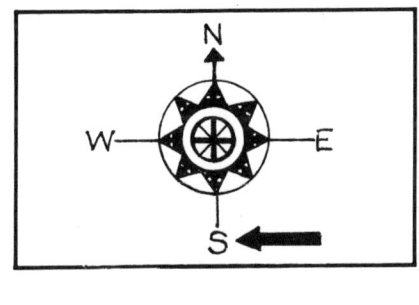 

play _ _ _ _ _ _ _   _ _ _ _ _   _ _ _ _ _ _

39

Draw these things.

a ship that has run aground	a man counting thousands of pounds	a rounders bat
a teacher shouting at you	a net bag full of sprouts	a thunder cloud
an underground tunnel	some children on a roundabout	a man getting out of prison
a little kangaroo peeping out of his mum's pouch	a clown with baggy trousers and a red mouth	Robin Hood in his green outfit

40

Read these words.

foul   playground   layabout   around   found   clouds
out   mouth   wound   bloodhound   count   pounds

Now write them in these gaps.

1. A person who never does a thing is called a _____.

2. The clock stopped because it was not _____ up.

3. If it is not lost, it must be _____.

4. A _____ is very good at tracking down criminals.

5. If you are not in, you must be _____.

6. The referee will send you off if you commit a _____.

7. A very rich man has thousands of _____.

8. He is very silly. He never stops messing _____.

9. You can _____ on your fingers.

10. There are swings and roundabouts on the _____.

11. Thunder _____ are black.

12. You put food in your _____.

41

This is a brown trout. It has a long, round body with lots of brownish red spots. These spots blend in with the background of the river bed, so the trout is very difficult to see.
The trout loves to catch fat insects in its big mouth. It can leap several feet out of the water to get at them. Trout are found living in very fast streams and rivers. Fishermen love to get trout on their hooks. A lucky fisherman may catch a trout of ten pounds or more.

1. What is this fish called?

___

2. Why is it difficult to see?

___

3. What does it love to eat?

___

4. Are trout good at jumping?

___

ar

Colour this.

Write.

ar   ar   ar   ar   ar   ar

___   ___   ___   ___   ___   ___

g**ar**den

All these words have **ar** in them. Can you read them?

1. farmer   2. scar   3. cart   4. park   5. target   6. arm

Draw them in these boxes.

1.	2.	3.
4.	5.	6.

Add **ar** to finish these words.

p __ __ don   sn __ __ l   b __ __   sm __ __ t   h __ __ d

__ __ ch

Can you read them to the teacher?

Write the words. The dashes will help you.

_ _ _ _   _ _ _   _ _ _ _ _ _ _

_ _ _ _   _ _ _ _   _ _ _

_ _ _ _ _   _ _ _ _   _ _ _ _ _

_ _ _ e _   _ _ _ _   _ _ _ _ e _

_ _ _ _ _   _ _ _   _ _ _ _ _

Draw these things.

a farmer's cart full of hay	an alarm clock with big bells on top	some cars in a car park
a shark with sharp teeth	some animals in a farmyard	an archer shooting at a target
a footmark in yellow sand	a party hat	a pack of cards
a teacher marking a book	an artist with his easel	a starfish on the beach

Read these words.

ark   start   marks   farm   barks   tartan
hard   cards   march   Mars   jar   Sharks

Now write them in these gaps.

1. My dog _____ very loudly.

2. These sums are too _____ for me.

3. The teacher _____ our books.

4. _____ is called the red planet.

5. Scotsmen have _____ kilts.

6. Get the _____ out so that we can play 'Snap'.

7. My dad was angry because his car would not _____ .

8. _____ live in the sea.

9. In the army, they teach you to _____ .

10. Cows, pigs and sheep are _____ animals.

11. The animals went two by two into the _____ .

12. My mum sent me to the shop to fetch a _____ of jam.

This is a barn owl. It has big eyes and a beak like a hook. The barn owl sleeps all day. It goes hunting in the dark as its big eyes help it to see very well in the darkness. It swoops across grasslands, farmlands and marshes, looking for something to eat. It kills pests like rats, but it can catch fish too. Farmers like barn owls to live in their barns because they kill pests. The mum owl lays between three and seven eggs in May. The little owls are called owlets, and at first they are very fluffy. This fluff is called down. As soon as the owlets get bigger, the adult owls will teach them how to hunt.

1. Why does the barn owl have big eyes?

_____

2. Why do farmers like barn owls?

_____

3. What are little owls called?

_____

4. What is down?

_____

 As soon as you can read **Words 3** at the back, you can go on to read '**The snagron**'.

Words 1   These are for **The trip**.

again   be   cave   was   long   me

before   eyes   eyelids   here   no   were

day   I   began   beginning   their   by

no-one   nobody   would   said   could   stopped

Ben's   It's   Let's   Windbag's

Words 2   These are for **The Glen of Gloom**.

answer   came   didn't   gone   head

like   mouth   hissed   queen   looked

my   question   want   sound   tail

water   saw   tongue   your   seemed

cave's   snagron's   that's

Words 3   These are for **The snagron**.

don't   hide   when   able   made

I'll   any   door   which   other

asked   who   time   fork   I'm

knew   sky   many   towards   above

chief's   Freddy's   Hilda's

She's   There's   What's   Where's

48

Oxford
University
Press